Returning

A THESIS

by David Widup

ALSING RESERVOIR PRESS • ASHLAND, OREGON

Returning: A Thesis

by David Widup

© 2019 David Widup

Published by Alsing Reservoir Press, Ashland Oregon

All rights reserved. No part of this book may be used or reproduced by any means without the written permission of the author except in the case of brief quotations embodied in critical articles and reviews.

Book design: booksavvystudio.com
Cover photo: pexels.com

ISBN: 978-1-7337365-1-0

First Edition

Printed in the United States of America

Returning: A Thesis

Submitted to the Faculty and Academic Board of the

Master of Fine Arts Writing Program

Pacific University

Forest Grove, Oregon

by David Widup

in partial fullfillment of requirements for the degree of

Master of Fine Arts in Writing in Poetry

November 19, 2018

Approved:

Dorianne Laux, Advisor, MFA in Writing

Shelley Washburn, Director, MFA in Writing

Sarah Phillips, Dean, College of Arts & Sciences

Table of Contents

I. CREATIVE MANUSCRIPT:

    The Neighborhood of Suffering 1

II. CRITICAL ESSAY:

    Nightmare Geometry 55

III. BIBLIOGRAPHY:

    MFA in Writing Reading List 69

PART I
CREATIVE MANUSCRIPT

The Neighborhood of Suffering

Close to Death

> If I am close to death and life support would only postpone the moment of my death:
>
> INITIAL ONE:
>
> ____ I want to receive tube feeding.
>
> ____ I want tube feeding only as my physician recommends.
>
> ____ DO NOT WANT tube feeding.
>
> Oregon Health Decisions,

I don't know what it is to be close to death.
  Does that mean that it is nearby,
  and I can see it easily, without my glasses,
  or maybe it's not a space thing
  but a time thing and close to death means
  it could happen now,
  before punctuation gets put on the
  end of this line?

Or maybe, it is a course correction thing –
  close to death means I will die soon if I don't
  do something, like change course,
  veer hard left towards the center line,
  away from the ditch, sweat in my eyes
  another close call, one more.

I'm thinking there might be a death neighborhood,
  you know, across town,
  through the square with the nice shops,
  the Information Center stand with pamphlets
  the smiling old lady, the statue of the boy pissing
  in the fountain,
  past the park
  up on the hill.

Yes, that's where death is, up the hill,
   not down here in the suffering neighborhood
   by the railroad tracks and the wannabe parks
   built between the tracks and the hardware store,
   lumber yard and dog park and all the other places you
   never want to go, but have to
   from time to time,
   you know, for maintenance:
         change the light bulb,
            exercise the dog,
               fix the garage door.

What happens if someone thinks I'm close to death,
   you know, up the hill on the other side of the park,
   and I'm really just suffering and longing?
   Maybe I'm just at the hardware store being grumpy
   and silent because I hate to fix broken things,
   but I'm not close to dying, I feel OK, I'm just pissed because
   I'm doing stupid stuff. What happens if I'm
   doing maintenance and they think
   I'm close to death and pull the plug?
   The garage door doesn't get fixed,
   the light bulb stays burnt out and Nancy can't see
   when she walks downstairs for water in the middle
     of the night,
   Molly doesn't get her special dog treats and pouts
   when Mark comes and goes and can't give her something
   to let her know he loves her and will come back,
   take her outside and throw the ball when he gets here.
   What happens then?

Sometimes When I'm Alone

"I ain't never found no place for me to fit. Seem like all I do is start over. It ain't nothing to find no starting place in the world. You just start from where you find yourself."
 AUGUST WILSON, *Joe Turner's Come and Gone*

Dad was smart looking
in his blue officer's suit,
bars, ribbons and medals,
starch, creases sharp as a knife,
gig line straight, even.
His uniform an escarpment
between him and his world.
Like my house today,
full of books, music, clutter.

Mom needed to be home,
South Bend was a haven.
Mother, brother, lovers, friends
tugged at her heart, minute
to hours to days
for three decades
before the flood came.
Like my life now,
waiting, wanting.

We lived with this
peacock and puppy dog,
the gentleman vagabond
and his wife filled
with a yearning, hot
and simmering
right below the surface.
Wiesbaden, Alamogordo, Narimasu,
Orlando, Joliet, Rockaway.

Go, no stay.
Move, no sit.
Bright, sparkly things,
black storm clouds promising.
Coming and going.
Doing and being.
Push and pull.

Sometimes when I'm alone
I look at stars,
sink into the void,
falling, no floating.
I press my cheek against
a cold, stone wall
for relief,
some hard comfort.

Dwayne Gets Ready

Clean khakis and a collared shirt,
Dwayne showers and doesn't shave,
that old razor will surely hurt

his wrinkled face. In the mirror
he sees his eyes – yellow whites, blood
shot veins, bags. He sees clearer

and looks better with specs. Horn
rim or wires tonight, what's the look
that will fit? Want to avoid the scorn,

just this once, from the nasty souls
that make him squirm when he's doing
good. He picks wires. Socks without holes,

a nice touch, something to smile about, heading
down the stairs. It's good to feel together
when going out, it's not a big wedding

but a party just the same and Dwayne
needs this real bad, tonight, to be with others,
talk and laugh and dance, maybe drink Champagne.

February, Mother's Grave

My father gives me directions
from his mother's house
to the cemetery where

my mother lies waiting.
We are quiet, the way
strangers keep within.

Not finding her,
he goes into the office
to ask directions.

I listen to Bach, stare
through the bare branches.
He returns breathless, pale,

with a map,
an 'X' where mom should be.
He drives.

I take the map when he stops,
orient myself to mom
and walk to the site.

Below the grey sky,
we stand staring
at the tombstone.

He should have someone
care for the site he says.
I sweep dirt and twigs off the stone

with the sole of my boot.

Joe's Cup of Joe

It all started on a snowy night last February when Jim,
the guy that plows the streets around here
in Boothbay Harbor, Maine,
came around the corner too fast in his pickup truck
on his way, I am sure, to the Maintenance Yard on Main Street
just opposite Joe's Cup of Joe, where I am now sitting
drinking coffee with a grease stain floating on top,
grease I'm sure will clog my arteries and kill me some day,
just as dead as Jim is now,
buried up on the hill next to his Mom and Dad
and his son Jeremy, who bit the dust that same day,
but in a different place, up towards the dump,
two of them dead, buried the same day,
only Jim's wife left now, alone, working long hours
serving coffee and burgers at Joe's Cup of Joe,
watching the TV above the pass thru filled with plates,
the sound on mute, no
longer spending time with me.
    Imagine that.

Wedding Rings

I have a box of them,
all from this marriage,
not the others. Somewhere
is a ring from the
first, and none
from the second.
Was there even a ring?
There was a ceremony
in Malibu, people flew
in for it, a ring
must have made
an appearance.
Maybe Susan has it.

These rings are gold,
white gold,
black and gold,
gold with a diamond,
one is just plain black.
Thick and heavy
from its own gravity.

They're all round, that's the point,
right? The great circle of life,
what goes around comes around,
the circle of trust, the eternal cycle.
Not a line, with a beginning and
end. Not even an arc, leaning
gracefully forward,
a sweep in time,
more a recurring motion, than a thing.
I twirl the ring on my left hand,
this way, once, twice, then that way.
It is gold, with a squared top, the tiny
diamond off to one side.
Which side are you on?

Anniversary

47 years ago, today,
Custer threw imaginary rice,
Sonny tossed popcorn
that survived the prior
night's Kazoo Band
munchies.

Marie and I,
bride and groom,
freshly returned from our
destination wedding –
Kimball County courthouse
Nebraska, just miles
from the missile site
that was my home,
3 days on, 3 days off.

She was pregnant. I had
mono. We were broke.
Marriage was an answer
to a question that could
not quite form, an itch
no one could reach,
an unease that aroused
us, looking over each
other's' shoulder.

Get a Job

Bags of vermiculite,
soda ash or
cement mixer
one on top of another,
nine hours a day,
six days a week.
Sixty pounds per bag.

Dust everywhere,
under your fingernails,
mixed with sweat and, then -
a concrete factory
right there on
the end of your hand.

It dries and pulls the nail
away from your finger,
doesn't hurt much
at first. Then you see drops
of blood on your fingertips,
splatters on the factory floor.

Wipe it on your jeans,
pick up more dust for good measure,
lift a sixty-pound bag onto a pallet,
then another and another.
The nail separates more,
fingers outlined in blood.

The factory grinds,
dust fills the air, hoppers bang, pregnant
with powders dropped into sacks,
stitched shut with a whap, whap, whap.
They lie in waiting
for a pallet bed
crawling on the conveyor
belt, grinding away.

Wrap your fingers
in thin gauze tape,
put on a pair of latex gloves.
They tear with the next bag
thrown on the pallet.
Start over,
off with the latex gloves,
now in shreds,
off with the bloody gauze wrap
stuck on your fingers.

Your fingertip swells
like a bulb.
New latex gloves now,
and an old pair of canvas
gloves from the back.

They're stiff and it's
hard to grab the bags,
throw them on the pallet.
One bag every 20 seconds,
three each moment.
One gets past,
kick it off the belt.
Fingers throbbing,
back muscles sore,
you squeeze your hands
harder through stiff gloves,
lift the next bag off the belt,
slap it on the pallet.

You wipe sweat from your forehead
with the back of your forearm.
The foreman comes by,
says you're docked for the gloves
you're bleeding into.

Dwayne Goes to Work

Dwayne gets off the bus, limps and leans,
looking down at his torn sneakers.
Need replacements before rains come.

Frozen stiff in place, Dwayne stares
up, at the office door sign – "Voc.
Rehab." *Piece work - it's come to this.*

The bus snorts away, doors still closing
Dwayne cannot walk in, cannot leave.
Stuck again, he drowns in hunger.

Pride cloaks him, a heavy wet
blanket he carries – a birthmark
staring him down - the gun barrel.

A nickel for a stuffed letter,
A buck for twenty, lunch at the
Senior Center for a hundred.

I can do this, he pauses and Dwayne
steps to the doors, looks down.
A hundred letters – let's do it.

Me

of course, it's about me,
it couldn't be otherwise
I don't even know me
but I damn sure don't
know anyone else.

Not mom whose face
blends into my sister's,
my wives',
my own.
I think of Mom's
steely black
silver coal dust
hair, a tangle of confusion.
Confusing
even me.

Me. what is left
after all the crap hardens,
a thin shell
cracked, flaking, dust
on the floor. What is
left.

for gone,
    left to die
        naked
            scared, alone.

Numbers Song

Here are some real numbers,
true and accurate.
I attended 7 grade schools,
1 middle school,
3 high schools.
I was 18
when I landed in Bien Hoa,
almost 20
when I returned to Phan Rang.
I have 5 kids
with 3 women, plus
3 stepchildren. Somewhere
there are 9 grandkids.

I have lived, I think,
in 24 dwellings
in 11 states
and 6 countries.
I am not a gypsy
or a lost, wandering soul.
Mom died 50 years ago,
Dad 23 – he lived 27
years without her.
With luck, I'll double that.
How's your math
holding up?
Cec died the same year that
I put Ethel down, just 4
years ago. Grandma lived to
101 ½, most of it good time.

Honest, this wasn't my idea,
I don't even like numbers,
they have just done me in
over and over and over again.
I don't keep track, say
"Hey, this is my 25th dwelling
in my 12th state or
maybe 7th country."
I had to count them up
just now.
I wrote it all down once –
the dates, the places, the schools,
the deaths, the losses -
that was the last time
I almost had a drink.
What harm can 6 oz. of
13 proof Chardonnay do to my
AST and ALT scores?
Tell the truth,
I am.
How are your numbers?

Where I'm From

after George Ella Lyon

I am from a rollaway bed and plastic toy soldiers,
    from a bow and arrow of sticks and twigs.
I am from the back of the station wagon,
    light blue, split plastic seats, tobacco infused.
I am from the Sacred Gardens of Kyoto, quiet etched
    grounds, each step a whispered prayer -
    wandering alone, lost, hypnotized.

I am from a sweat stained, Epiphone fretboard and
    Winston cigarettes, from Runkle and Wilson
    and Peart blood.
I'm from drinking booze to numb the pain
    and tears of shame for what I have,
from *Don't lie to me!* and *We can't afford that*.
I'm from Evening Prayer, sung *a cappella*
    by children in a small stone chapel,
      "Let us Bless the Lord." "Thanks be to God."

I'm from Cec and Sherron and Uncle Skip and Aunt
    Margaret, from cinnamon toast for breakfast and
    pot roast on Sundays.
From the life my father tried to take, but failed,
my mother's - drowned in bourbon.

I have her torn leather notebook
    with yellowed pages, old and cracking,
    poems by others, notes of her own.
I am in her journal, it was kept for me -
    sadness on every page,
    hope between the lines.

Family Tree

Hemmingway wrapped wire
around the trigger, the other
end tied to his toe, put both
barrels in his mouth and
kicked his life away.
Drunk.

That first sweet sip,
the urge each day lying in bed,
a promise that lured me upright,
it has exacted its duty.

Uncle Skip went first, driving
to work drunk on Monday morning.
Then Mom married the bottle,
drowned in her vomit at 3 PM,
left Dad to figure it out.

Her parents, Clell and Mabel,
gave up after Mom's funeral.
Rocking back and forth on the old sofa,
eyes vacant, Grandma said,
"No parent should have to
bury all their children."
then moved on the next day.

My wife, finally sober, passed
in an Arizona halfway house,
asleep on the living room sofa,
alone, on the eve of the century.

A brother in a San Jose motel room,
gone at least a week when found,
dozens of empties on the floor,
under the bed, in his pockets.

My sister Cec, in the ICU,
finally sober, but wrecked,
tubes in her arms, out her groin,
lights too white, always on,
eyes begging for peace.

My oldest child passed out,
six-inch scalp gash, four hours
on a stairwell floor, blood
seeping, turning purple, then black.
"I can quit" he'd said that morning.

I don't know my family,
or even what a family is,
how to be a father, a husband.
The legacy of a tired life,
tied to the allure,
the cutting edge,
the numbing.

We live your dying
drunken torture
every day.

Dwayne Cries in His Beer

"I've been to Providence, lived in Bethlehem,
got the Northeast covered like my face.
Been there, done that, thank you please.

Painted homes in Truckee, camped in the Applegate.
No place feels like home, nowhere calls.
Some days don't seem to end."

The bartender sets another draft
 "You need a new story, Dwayne.
Nobody gives a shit about your unrest."

Dwayne holds the glass on the bar
tilts it left, then right, stares,
pours it all on the counter.

 "Nobody gives a shit about your bar,"
he mumbles as the beer creeps
down to the rail, forms a pool.

Dwayne is splashed as the bar rag
flies down in front of him.
"I wish you'd get a life, man."

I Had No Idea

Mom died - it was the beginning
of my journey to Vietnam.
She died alone, in her bed
on a hot July afternoon in 1967,
the summer before my Senior year,
in a suburban New Jersey house
without air conditioning.
I was in an Indiana book bindery.
We were both sweating at 3:30 PM
when she let out her last breath.

She hated the war. She loved me.
If she had lived, I wouldn't have gone.
I ran away that summer,
I didn't think it would kill her.
I can't get the image of her —
pale face with gray black hair
spilling onto the white pillow,
eyes barely shut, lips slightly apart —
out of my mind.
I cannot separate my going
to Vietnam from her death.

I joined the Air Force. I had no idea
they would give me a gun,
send me to Vietnam within a year.
I had no idea that at 18, I'd be in charge
of a small armory and security for
400 men and $25 million of equipment.
I had no idea, that day Mom died
as I looked up at the clock
on the shipping dock wall.
No idea at all.

Black and White

My image of Nam
before I got there
was black and white,
what I had seen on a TV set.

I thought about the war
as good guys, victims all,
fighting a miserable, foreign war.
Once *Life* had black and white
pictures of the men killed
in Vietnam the prior week.

I can remember every hour
between when I got orders to go
and touchdown at Bien Hoa.
Two months left at Altus AFB,
one month of leave, home,
two months of jungle training.
I still remember dreams of Canada,
but never figured out how.
I never thought it would happen.
It seemed so unreal, those long
five months.
I kept thinking I would
wake up.

Fifty Years Ago, Today
(18 SEP 68)
Rainbow, rainbow don't be blue
four more years and you'll be through
Am I right or wrong?

   5:00 AM
My father wakes me up.
I smell he's showered and shaved,
wonder again how he
never seems to sleep.

There's grey light outside my window.
I hear the birds, a car every so often.
I get out of bed,
dead man rising from the grave.
He drives me to Newark,
the Armed Forces Induction Center.
We don't talk as we pass yellow
school buses with black lettering
moving to their first pick up.
High School kids at the foot of the hill,
smoking cigarettes, laughing.
I know nothing,
nothing at all.
I light another cigarette.

My father listens to classical music
as we drive Routh 46 East.
His uniform fits him well,
I wonder about the ribbons on his chest.
He is silent, retired eight years
now. I was prouder of him
when he wore a uniform every day.
I would never tell him that.

10:30 AM
My father swears me in.
We stand as a group, thirty or forty
young men in jeans and long hair
pledge to love, honor and obey.
Tired and confused, he looks at
me as he administers
the time-honored oath
to serve, honor, protect,
he looks at me
as if he's never seen me before.

1:00 PM
My father is in my thoughts,
his wet steel eyes still
staring at me being inducted,
as I get another physical,
strange men squeezing
my balls, putting their middle finger
up my asshole too far,
for too long.
I wonder if he knows
this is happening to his oldest son.

11:00 PM
My father is absent, again,
late that night, standing in
the spotlight with my squad -
79 new companions.
They are quiet now, shifting
from foot to foot. I'm sweating,
even though it's getting cold.
I hear him before I see
my Drill Sargent's black face
under a dark olive, Smokey the Bear hat,
above a facade of starched khakis:

"LISTEN UP MOTHERFUCKERS.
*WHAT I'M ABOUT TO TELL YOU
MAY SAVE YOUR ASS!*"

In My Bones

I can't recall not having
the war in my bones.
It's like looking in a story book.
I recognize the people and faces -
Graduation Day,
the last day at the plastic bottle factory,
my trip to Tennessee,
even Boot Camp.
I recognize them all, but I can't
feel me in them.
I didn't exist before the war,
now I carry it with me
           wherever I go,
                all the time.

When I get tired I get blown away.
I don't see the things I need to see,
I forget to watch where I put my boots down,
miss that small flash ten clicks out.
I overlook an old woman's
glance as she passes -
black teeth,
black hair,
black pajamas,
black death.

 The first months, I couldn't keep food
down. I gave up booze and
just smoked—cigarettes and dope.
I sold liquor rations to lifers,
used the money to buy weed.
Money for nothin' .... weed for free.

RETURNING ~ A THESIS ~ David Widup

The beauty of Vietnam –
the blue, warm sheen of the South China Sea,
the black sky highlighting a huge moon
laying low on the runway,
some nights big as an erupting dawn.
The dense, green mountains west of Phan Rang,
trees and ferns. I swear, I heard
Charlie with the wind in those trees.
Sometimes quiet and calm
unlike any place I've ever been.

I was a happy self-sufficient animal.
The longer in country, the happier.
Until the end
when I faced the streams of sewage
and rage that collected,
every day, each step,
the walking breath,
the images and moments burned.

Details pull the trigger, drag
me back into hell. It takes a crazy
person to pull them out, maggots
in a rotted corpse,
put them on a page,
make them real again –
for all the world to see and smell.

I have made myself sick
writing about Vietnam.
And I haven't really started.

Short Timer

My squadron was unusual –
we went over together
were all short together –
> *so short we needed a ladder to climb up onto a dime,*
> *so short we had to look up to look down, able to finish,*
> *need to take a crap, but don't want to miss my plane,*
> *want to smoke a cigarette, but don't want to waste it.*

Short was less than 100 days left
in country. Short meant FIGMO.
Short timers had their own culture,
their own set of rules.
Some slept in bunkers,
afraid the first rocket in would catch them sleeping.
Many stopped booze and drugs.
Those that had started out fucking
worried about the clap and VD.
Everyone who was going to take R&R had.
There was nothing left looking forward
but home.

I was crazy
I was sure I was going to die.
I was stoned most of the time,
flew an airplane for kicks,
went up in a Huey gunship
in the middle of a rocket attack.

I was sure I was going to die.
I thought about extending
for another seven months,
but didn't.
I quit writing home.
I mostly hurt from head to toe –
afraid to stay and afraid to go.

Bien Hoa to Tokyo

i

We're all headed home, bags under our eyes as dark and almost as big as the duffels we dragged when we boarded, just as the sun came up.

Last night I slept on the ground. I dreamed I was flying above the base, arms outstretched

gliding on air, close enough to the ground to see the people walking, the planes on the runway,

trucks coming and going, guys lined up like a long snake, headed further in country. Soaring.

Soaring, that's what I was doing. Dreaming taught me to soar. Dreaming taught me the body is less than a dream.

ii

Jimmy Scarpatti and I sit together, an old 707, but at least it has real seats that recline and stewardesses -

the best-looking women I have seen in 366 days, that's for sure - to bring food and water. But they send out vibes to leave them alone. Whatever...

We've been together for a year and I don't know him. He's from Brooklyn, smiles a lot, drinks little, stays out of the way.

I don't sleep on airplanes, he says, before we take off. Just so you know. I'll just sit here and read and smoke. Maybe have a shot or two. You?

No, I don't sleep much on planes either. I don't have anything to do but get there. Along for the ride.

Jimmy's by the window, I'm on the aisle. How long's the flight I ask. Bien Hoa, Tokyo, Anchorage, McGuire.

Long time. Depends. Could be a day, maybe more.
    When will we get there? What day will it be? No clue.

Jimmy looks out the window as we turn onto the runway, I don't even know what
    day it is there now.

Rolling, nose up, wheels up. I wait for a blast or explosion. Still shaking and trying
    to hide it, chain smoking,

waiting for the end. Just the whoosh of the long jetliner aimed upward. Dodged another one, I think.

What're you going home to? Jimmy asks. My vision is closing in, my head started to throb when we took off. I'm off to Francis E. Warren next.

That's in Colorado, huh? Wyoming, I say. Wyoming. Shit.
    Is that a place? My mind is sore. I can't think of anything to say.

iii

Jimmy says, I don't care about this, I'm getting out when we get back.
    I'm so short I need a ladder to climb up on a dime.

How much time you got left? I tell him two years. Two years? You're still green.
    Whistle britches. The stewardess comes on the PA:

> *no smoking in the aisles or bathroom, only drink what we give you,*
>   *water, coffee,*
>
> *soda pop, we'll confiscate any open hooch that you brought on board,*
>   *no food in flight,*
>
> *in Tokyo and Anchorage you can buy food, the stewardesses have the*
>   *last word,*
>
> *any violation of these rules and you will be detained at the next stop and*
>   *returned to Bien Hoa,*
>
> *handed over to the Military Police for processing. Welcome home.*
>   *Thank you for your service.*

What are you going back to Jimmy? My father wants me to join the family
    business, he says. The plane banks hard and I see the ocean out the window.

The jet engines speed and shriek, my hand starts to shake. I'm confused, haven't
    felt anything in some time.

I get up to go to the latrine after we level off. The PA barks *No smoking in the aisle way*! I sit down again.

Jimmy chuckles. Imagine that, we wander around the jungle for a year building towers and runways out of nothing, trying not to get killed

by teenagers with submachine guns, have our wives and girlfriends dump us and now we're being talked to like we're in first grade.

Butt in the ashtray, I head back to the latrine.

Coming Home

I came home but didn't get out.
When I landed at Ft. Dix that muggy
September night in 1970,
I had two years left.
Depositing two cigarette packs
full of "The World's Best Grass"
in the Amnesty Box,
I took off my jungle fatigues,
put them in the trash can,
put on civilian clothes.
I was clean and sober,
felt hungover and numb.
It was a black night,
thunderstorms without lightening.

I dozed in someone's car
all the way to my sister's
in New York City, still dark, wet.
I just sat and looked at them.
I didn't know what to say.
They seemed strange to me.
I felt their anticipation
with every breath.
I don't remember what was said,
though we talked until dawn.

In a laundromat that week,
I remember being ashamed,
how stunning,
beautiful, the women were.
I remember being
dirty, unworthy.
They looked at me,
question marks, scorn.

RETURNING ~ A THESIS ~ David Widup

Coming home is hard.
I've been doing it most my life, and
still haven't gotten it right.

Back in the World

I was at Woodstock
"An Aquarian Exposition"
on leave, mostly stoned,
before being dumped
in Bien Hoa
three weeks later.

Back in the World,
New York City,
September 1970
I saw the film
Woodstock: 3 Days of Peace and Music
with my sister, Cec -
a weekday matinee.

Outside, hot and humid,
like Vietnam
with more noise.
Inside, dark and cold,
hell's thermostat
gone awry. Buttered
popcorn cool before we sat.
I watched and watched,
searching for something familiar -
the mud-pit, the camp sites filled
with babies and pot and
the Grateful Dead and
that low white noise hum.
I did not see anything,
not one thing
in three hours,
I could recall.
It was not there.
I wasn't the same,
Cec and I were not the same.

Dwayne Falls for Saigon

Choppers land on the Embassy
roof covered with people,
on a TV behind plate glass.

Dwayne blinks, squints,
checks his watch, looks up.
One lifts off, a person hanging

from the open cargo door.
On the roof, arms stretch up -
to reach or to push down?

His eyelids droop as Dwayne recalls
the mass of people on the roof,
the stairwell packed, smelling of fear.

There was no place to put them, no
space for them. The choppers
stopped, the line of people didn't.

"You OK, man?" Dwayne wipes
his coat sleeve on his face. Turns -
helping or pushing down?

The King and I

The king and I dance this dying game,
I stand beside him, He sits inside me,
And, sometimes, I forget who to blame.

The land is barren, the animals gone lame,
On the throne, his scepter across his knees.
The king and I dance this dying game.

I run to my liege, calling his name,
"Make it better", I scream as a banshee,
And, sometimes, I forget who to blame.

Going inside, I pledge to his fame,
I beg him to act, to look and to see.
The king and I dance this dying game.

I'm shaking and cold, no fires or flame.
I must act now, consummate my glory,
And, sometimes, I forget who to blame.

A breath, a blink, my hand takes aim,
And the king in me shoots him, or is it me?
The king and I dance this dying game,
And, sometimes, I forget who to blame.

Where'd You Come From, Dwayne?

Blue tape and a two-inch chip brush,
from Flat Black coffee and Sinatra's cashmere voice.
and New England clapboard houses -

stubborn, musty, never quite clean.
… from Quaking Aspens in Colorado,
leaves dancing like a neon snow.

Sunday Mass, dinners at 5:30 PM
and booze. From Dwayne Sr., who left
before I came and Eloise who stayed, waiting.

… that quiet house with cold dark rooms,
from *if you want something, get it
yourself* and *no one likes a whiner.*

Spirits and gods, watching over
me, golds and silvers shaking
fore and around, bands of light.

I'm from Irish blood and fermented ire,
corned beef with cabbage and carrots
and red beer for breakfast.

… the brother who drowned
alone in Walden Pond at 18. Always,
dark circles under blue eyes.

We had pictures in the house,
collected on the wall of shame.
Forced smiles and pinched brows,

black and white or color,
the pain the same.
It seems like a graveyard now.

But for Fear

But for fear, I have felt little for years.
I know the knots and acid in my gut,
I hear ringing and tin noise in my ears.

It comes up on me fast, a dark lead flash,
My lips and chin tremble, I lose my breath,
Thoughts smolder and burn, my head is trashed.

I would do anything to cleanse myself
Of this curse, rid my brow of the dripped sweat
That burns my eyes. I wish I had a shelf

To put the fear on, sliding it
Like a cartridge between two books -
The Odyssey and *East of Eden.*

Foretelling a change, an end to the tears.
But for fear, I have felt little for years.

Rock Lake

One mile
across, one mile back.
At first, I kept looking up
to see the landmarks -
the boathouse over, my house back.
Later, I just swam, the warm water
caressing me, my arms,
my chest, between my legs.

My sister and I sat in the water
on hot, humid Florida afternoons.
The water to our waists,
we talked and sat and looked.
I was scared, she was lonely,
until the tables turned.

Up the sandy lakeshore,
across the maidencane and knotweed,
surrounded by crabgrass
our red clay patio held white
wrought iron table and chairs,
Mom sat there smoking, sipping
bourbon and sweating. Waiting
to explode.

In the ICU

My sister lays in a bed,
large hose down her throat,
mouth held open with a large plastic "O,"
her arms an octopus
of needled tubes.
Monitors on metal arms
flash numbers and lines,
humming, beeping
through the glare.

Her eyes are mostly closed,
vacant when open,
tear from time to time,
plead *Let me go.*
A selfish request, this,
but how can I say "No?"
How can I say "Yes?"
Her gaze goes into a
blank space, out of the ICU.

What is most intense
is the light,
bright white light,
always on.
There is no night or day,
dusk and dawn are gone.
The ICU
is a luminary assault,
a never-ending day.

I think of her garden at home,
green and rocky and wild,
the smell of dried grasses
and summer wildflowers
in my nose, earthen air

around me, in me.
This is her ashes' home.
Not in the ICU that's
bright, even in the darkness.

Fragments Found Inside My Sister

after Nick Flynn

i

On the side of the road
    in my pink dress, waiting
To be saved, by someone, anyone.
    A young sailor stopped and smiled,
helped Dad fix the flat, took a $5 bill
    winked and hopped into his truck.

ii

Invisible, that's what I was. Without form, I
    pushed a finger through myself.
I swam across Rock Lake and back,
    two miles, but only for myself.
Wanting to stop and rest, I swam on,
    wanting to ride the crest home.

iii

Those kids, like chicks with open mouths,
    Never full, there was not enough
Food, love, money, truth, stuff, stuff -
    a cacophony now, my ears hurt.
I took care of them, made it right
    held them dear in the cold, cold night.

iv

Indiana farm houses were the best,
    we laid in bed and kissed and slept.
Her touch was electricity. Shot from
    crown to groin. Summer breezes scant reprieve.
Opening my eyes was hard, hard
    taking in her long hair and painted eyes.

v

I just wanted to be a girl
    and to be loved.
I tasted lemon juice and honey
    only together, never apart.
My homes were frail, quaking, vacant
    like peace or Mom.

vi

My throat hurts. I cannot sleep.
    I am worn smooth and soft.
I chose this life and now
    it's time to go.
I'm tired,
    let me go.

Time

Later,
much later,
we decided
when
and how
to end
her life.
I'm not
over it, yet.
Time has a way…

I smell the soft perfume she used to wear,
back when she still cared. It's like
she's still here. I hope
I'm not holding her back.
Time has a way…

This peach has such a thin skin, it tears
with a light touch, and under
is that sweet, wet fruit, the good
stuff. It's on my
fingers, face, forearms,
moving, covering. This seed,
hard, sharp, bitter,
the source of all.

Time.
It has this way of caving in
on itself, a nuclear implosion.

Memories.

Holding the pick-up-sticks in my fist,
opening fingers, sticks splay
with a clatter.
Events jumble -
was it the blue or red
stick that moved last time?

Last to Know

GEICO just called,
Mark hit a pedestrian with the truck
either yesterday or three weeks ago,
they're not sure.
News to me.

My sister called,
Mom died,
not sure at home or where,
last night or maybe this morning,
had been sick for weeks.
News to me.

Sherron called,
my sister was in ICU,
cardiac arrest from complications,
maybe the heart or could be the liver,
just had surgery at Columbia Presbyterian.

Orders home came in,
going to Wyoming
or maybe its Colorado
doesn't matter, out West
away from my family.
News to me.

I'm the last to know
because there is nothing worth knowing
or maybe I'm not worth telling
or maybe the news just doesn't matter,
although I wonder if Mark hurt
the pedestrian,
I'm not sure.

Dwayne and Omar on the Park Bench

Dwayne and Omar, on the bench, in the park.
The sky is grey, rain drops, dusk is on them.
Omar asks, "Man why you bein' a snark?"

Before, Dwayne was a paycheck. He made
money, honey, knew how to make a mark.
Paid the bills, picked up the tab, made the grade.

He became "The Man" and he wore it well.
Now, he's a nobody, and he's afraid
of what he's become, can't ring the bell.

Dwayne crosses his arms and looks to the sky.
Says, "I got nothin' to give, nothin' to tell."
He wonders if its lost now, gone bye-bye.

or if, perhaps, it will make a return.
Maybe, God will just once, cast a blind eye.
Oh to be "The Man" again, stop this churn.

Enough! Enough for now. It's getting dark.
Sometimes a day is just a page to turn.
Dwayne and Omar, on the bench, in the park.

Nowhere

I live in the middle of nowhere. Actually, it is not nowhere, it's
    no-where, as in not near anyplace people tend to go,

unless they are lost and looking for somewhere to get found.
    But then, when they get here, they think

they are close to where they need to be, because when they are
    here they are not nowhere, they are here

and that is better than not being anywhere, I'm thinking.
    The hills outside my windows are green all year, that's a blessing --

to be able to see life even in the dead of winter when most things are.
    The bears are sleeping,

the leaves have fallen off the trees, the flowers are dead stalks in a hard,
    cold soil that won't give up

anything, anywhere. I put my head in the pine covered hills to sleep and
    lift it out in the morning.

The smell is sandalwood musk. Green. My daughter says that this place is
    idyllic, magical, mystical, almost perfect.

The soft verdant hillside, the silence at night and all the people that aren't
    here, but are there, wherever that is.

What more could you ask for? - her question that hangs in the air.

Songs

Ready to rock and roll
with Kahuna 3.0
All the way down town, man
downtown, all the way
down. Go down, fall
through the floor, fall
through the ceiling, fall
through the walls, rock bottom,
downtown, down to the pound.

Now, let's be clear,
there is honesty being spoken now—
real and, therefore, true.
It can't be false or made up,
where would it come from,
thin air? gasses and fumes? spirits?
It didn't just end up in my head,
magically one moment.
The monsters with legs of eels
and flashing red eyes,
those did not just get deposited
in the checking account of my soul,
a surprise wire transfer
from God.
I don't think so.
The monsters are real,
they cannot be imaginary.
No more pretending.

OK, so some things
are a little muddled,
not to the letter of the law.
Forgive me judge,
I have exaggerated.
But even an exaggeration
cannot be all made up.
I am not exalting vapor,
I am yelling reality
so that it can be seen,
clearly, like the bottom of a sparkling
sunlit shallow swimming pool,
the water in the pool magnifies
the beauty of the blue stones below,
like my soul magnifies God's glory.
It's not make believe, it's like sperm
invading the wall of an egg under a
microscope—it's real even though
it's not apparent. It's not make believe.
There, if you still doubt me, Santa
brings presents for Christmas,
the Tooth Fairy puts quarters
under pillows, the stork delivers
babies and Jesus is in love,
maybe in love with you,
right now,
today, here.
Jesus loves you.

Some songs are blast real—
under an examination light without
grace. Some, I'm not sure which,
maybe not so stark real, but
in the vicinity.

RETURNING ~ A THESIS ~ David Widup

Maybe not in the same Zip code, but
definitely, definitely in the same
area code. One SMSA for real songs
and almost real songs. Some songs,
maybe more, are the right notes,
just the order has changed –
same key, different tune.
Kind of like singing "Get Back"
to the tune of "Gimme Shelter."
Others, well maybe I got the key
wrong. I'm not perfect –
that's the truth.
C Major and G Major are close,
that's easy to fake and it's still real.
E Minor – now that's a
big exaggeration. I mean
if it is a G Major poem
we're talking commanding,
bright highs and solid mid-range,
a statement – I am here
you hear? Got it, dude?
E Minor is a requiem in
a song, bury me, throw the
dirt on top, say a prayer, move on.
Once E Minor comes to town,
hide the children, pay the bills
and get ready to die, damn it.

So, here's the issue – I'm not
entirely sure what is true
and what is in the same
area code and what is a small
change in notes within a key,
what is a change in key and

what is a new tune with
altered lyrics all together.
I mean I think I know it,
but only after it is sung,
and even then, I'm not so sure –
anyway, it is not deception, that's
what I'm trying to say –
it's not deception, it's confusion,
exhaustion, limbs like weights,
heart fallen deep into my belly,
I just get confused when I'm tired
and I'm exhausted now to where
I just need to sit a few,
maybe get a cup, maybe rest my eyes
but only for a second or two.
I promise

PART II
CRITICAL ESSAY

Nightmare Geometry

Nightmare Geometry:
Soldiers Writing the Vietnam War

"After a while, the Vietnam War story became so jumbled and ambiguous, it was not a narrative at all. It was a kind of nightmare geometry. And it overwhelmed and undermined everything." — Kathryn Marshall

Introduction

The Vietnam War shaped generations, across the globe and in ways that we are still uncovering. The first war to be broadcast broadly on television, the Vietnam experience has been artistically explored most extensively in the visual arts – initially with films, but also television, paintings and sculptures. Writing about Vietnam has been largely fiction, albeit often autobiographical fiction or memoirs masked as novels. The literary exploration of the Vietnam experience has been sporadic and continues to evolve, even now, over 40 years after the fall of Saigon.

Two works that stand out are Yusef Komunyakaa's *Dien Cai Dau* and Tim O'Brien's lyric book of linked stories, *The Things They Carried*. These two collections share common threads that transcend the shared experiences of American soldiers in the Vietnam War. Most importantly they also share a commitment to artistic craft. There are three important ways that Komunyakaa and O'Brien display their craft and show the courage to explore and lay bare the raw and strange experiences that are the essence of the Vietnam War – language, psychic distance and point of view.

Yusef Komunyakaa, Tim O'Brien and I were in Vietnam at the same time, 1969 – 1970, and in many of the same villages, provinces and military zones. We may have been together at times: we all experienced Tết 1970 – the fury after months of quiet, with chaotic skirmishes and surreal images. We were all drenched in the monsoons that followed, some of the wettest and longest storms ever in that region. Everything was wet, all the time – toe rot, crotch rot, "cap crap" under helmeted heads. We walked hunched over, heavy ponchos with rain dripping off in sheets. We may have seen Bob Hope together on Long Binh, with Neil Armstrong and Miss World 1970. In all likelihood, we all landed at Tan Son Nhut, in-processed in the heat on the tarmac in one hour and were put on a chopper or in a truck for transport to our first duty station. Riding through Saigon, we probably all wondered, *Where is the enemy?* and *What is that awful smell?*

"Very Crazy" Language

Dien Cai Dau by Yusef Komunyakaa was first published in 1988. It was his fifth book of poetry in print. By that time, Komunyakaa was already an established poet. He was in Vietnam from 1969 to 1970 as a journalist in the U. S. Army. The title is taken from a Vietnamese phrase often translated as "crazy, behaving in strange and odd ways." The book is organized in a chronological manner, though it is not clear what poems are autobiographical, which ones are reported on and those that are imagined or created anew. The later poems are concerned with the traumas of coming home, the aftermath and the human toll that remains a lasting legacy.

As was typical in the Vietnam War, the language below the language is where much of the context is held. The phrase "dien cai dau" was used by Vietnamese to describe American soldiers behaving irrationally (often drunk, stoned or both) and by Americans to describe Vietnamese actions and situations that they did not understand. Metaphorically, "Dien cai dau" was the bizarre experience that Vietnam was to American military who served there. It was a phrase that rolled off tongues as an adjective, an adverb, a general sense of confusion and malaise. In reality, there were several languages used and misused in Vietnam by Americans - two dialects of Vietnamese (traditional and "modern"), French and English. The popular phrase used by Americans "Beaucoup dien cai dau" (meaning very crazy) is a blend of French, traditional and modern Vietnamese. Layer on the normal military jargon that soldiers predictably invent in their native language, and the result is the language of the American Vietnam War soldier.

The unique role of the language developed during the Vietnam War is fully displayed in Komunyakaa's *Dien Cai Dau*. Language is one key to why these poems are so powerful, unique and relevant. His poetic style tends towards rich vernacular enhanced with a lyric cadence and rhythm – perfect for the war fought by men who made up their own language to describe a war whose musical score includes "What's Going On?', "Gimme Shelter" and "Smokestack Lightnin'". His larger, characteristically vivid, evocative language is found throughout the book. In "Tunnels" he writes:

> He moves as if trying to outdo
>
> blind fish easing toward imagined blue,
>
> pulled by something greater than life's
>
> ambitions.

"A Greenness Taller than Gods" opens with the lines:
> When we stop,
>
> a green snake starts again
>
> through deep branches.
>
> Spiders mend webs we marched into.

> Monkeys jabber in flame trees,
>
> dancing on the limbs to make
>
> fire-colored petals fall.

The images are clear and unique, the language deceptively simple and the grounding in natural elements is apparent.

There are two other layers of language at play in these poems. The first concerns the unique collection of images, objects and events associated with the Vietnam War. In "Tunnels", a recounting of a Viet Cong tunnel search, there is the "tunnel rat, the smallest man", "the stench of honey buckets", pails of human and animal feces that were used to fertilize fields, coat punji sticks to kill and pollute abandoned tunnels, and "booby traps". In "Report from the Skull's Diorama" there is "Firebase San Juan Hill", "chopper blades", the "napalmed hill" and "AK-47s". These objects uniquely conjure specific aspects of Vietnam, in the language that was used in country by Americans. Komunyakaa uses these objects throughout the poems as footings to keep the poem in 1969 Vietnam.

The other layer is the language actually spoken. In the poetry of Dien Cai Dau, the spoken word is conveyed in dialogue, narration and reflection. In "Fragging" there is this talk of who will kill the Squadron leader:

> We won't be wasting a real man.
>
> That lieutenant's too gung ho.
>
> Think, man, 'bout how Turk
>
> got blown away; next time
>
> it's you or me. Hell,
>
> the truth is the truth.

And in "A Break from the Bush", an infantryman on an In-Country R&R:

> .... Can you see me now?
>
> In this spot they gonna build
>
> a Hilton. Invest in Paradise.
>
> Bang, bozos! You're dead.

The language in the dialogue relays the story, the setting and the narrator. It is clear, simple, direct and, consequentially, very powerful - it lingers. The combined effect from Komunyakaa's language – his unique poetic voice, phrases and semantics unique to the Vietnam War and dialogue that brings in the speaker, is to provide the canvas for each person to read and experience in their own way.

Tim O'Brien published a collection of linked short stores in 1990 titled *The Things They Carried*. The stories are openly autobiographical and, given their style and tone, seem to cross between fiction, memoir, poetry, autobiography and confessional essay. A key aspect of O'Brien's style is his careful use of spoken and narrative language registers, utilized in a manner similar to Komunyakaa. Not nearly as lyrical as *Dien Cai Dau*, O'Brien's book is sustained in part by a cadence and rhythm – a predictable repetition. In the title story, the phrase "They carried ..." appears over 100 time in 20 pages. It is used to describe objects (including weight and size), the soldiers' inventory of weaponry, personal effects that relate a story about the character, fears that they carried inside and things that carried the soldiers, real or imagined.

At times, O'Brien inundates the reader with jargon, but in a context that render the objects real, even when not familiar. In the same story, he writes: "They used a hard vocabulary to contain the terrible softness. *Greased* they'd say. *Offed, lit up, zapped while zipping.* It wasn't cruelty, just stage presence." Earlier in that story, he writes: "They carried USO stationary and pencils and pens. They carried Sterno, safety pins, trip flares, signal flares, spools of wire, razor blades, chewing tobacco, liberated joss sticks, candles, grease pens, the *Stars and Stripes*, fingernail clippers, Psy Ops leaflets, bush hats, bolos and much more." The effect of the language and rhythm is to put the reader there, in that space. It seems real. Both writers use jargon to open the door and welcome the reader into their uniquely weird world.

The parallels between the two writers' use of language holds with dialogue as well. Narration and authentic dialogue are strengths of O'Brien's. Here for example is an exchange between two soldiers after one returns from a tunnel search in which his companion dies:

> Like cement, Kiowa whispered in the dark. I swear to God – boom, down. Not a word.
> I've heard this, said Norman Bowker. A pisser, you know? Still zipping himself up.
>   Zapped while zipping.
> All right, fine. That's enough. Yeah, but you had to see it, the guy just –
> I *heard*, man. Cement. So why not shut the fuck *up*?

Language is what Yusef Komunyakaa and Tim O'Brien use to make the American soldiers' Vietnam understandable and familiar, while retaining its strange, surrealistic aura.

The Vietnam War was a stark contrast to what was expected and trained for. It was very real while being unbelievable, horrific and strange. Language is a door Komunyakaa and O'Brien used to make it believable and even more real. The language is authentic, specific to the experience in a relatable manner. The colloquial and idiomatic language, often revealing and shocking, provides dramatic realism that drives these collections.

Psychic Distance – "Don't Say Real Shit to the Civilians"

Psychic distance manages and controls the closeness to the narrator and their worldview. This is also termed "narrative distance", especially in describing fiction. While the coupling of psychic distance and point of view gives each poem a unique "voice" or "signature", they are separate levers that influence the literary experience in different ways.

In writing about the Vietnam War, Komunyakaa and O'Brien made choices about psychic distance and these choices reflected the experience of the author, the narrator and assumptions about the reader. A very close distance, where the narrator's thoughts and emotions are what is written, is intimate and demands all that intimacy does in terms of trust, an empathetic posture. This creates a shared experience, a sense of community, that brings the reader fully into the narrator's life. On the other hand, a removed distance makes the narrator almost a stranger. The narrator's inner world is not revealed. The Vietnam War, filled with strange images, sounds, smells and language was a challenging place to bring home to a someone who had not experienced it. How Komunyakaa and O'Brien handle this has much to do with the success of their writing about the Vietnam War.

The opening poem in Dien Cai Dau, "Camouflaging the Chimera", has the narrator describing in an objective manner how soldiers prepared for a patrol. The language is "straight talk" and the tone is distant:

> We tied branches to our helmets.
>
> We painted our faces & rifles
>
> with mud from a riverbank,

Even when Komunyakaa's inevitable poetic view enters the poem, it is still holding the reader at arm's length:

> We weren't there. The river ran
>
> through our bones. Small animals took refuge
>
> against our bodies; we held our breath,

Had this arms-length distance been maintained throughout the book, it could have been static and one-dimensional – a poetry war journal travelogue. But Komunyakaa quickly begins to close the distance, to make it personal, to bring it near. Just two poems later, he introduces a new psychic pose – personal, unsure, questioning. From "Somewhere Near Phu Bai":

> If I hear a noise
>
> will I push the button
>
> & blow myself away?
>
> The moon grazes treetops. I count the Claymores again.

> Thinking about buckshot
> kneaded in the plastic C-4
> of the brain, counting
> sheep before I know it.

We are drawn into the inner thoughts, doubts and specifics of the soldier's world here. Unlike the prior poem, with its reporting tone, this piece is an insider's view of the experience. He is not telling us what it's like, he is sharing the noise, his fear, the War's irony. The pattern of straight talk reporting (personal, but arms-length nonetheless) to reveal inner feelings and confusions is used throughout *Dien Cai Dau*. The effect is to inform and then reveal repeatedly. In consecutive poems, we shift from lines such as "It's more, man. Your money bought my new Chevy." (49) to "All the close calls / are inside my head / bright as a pinball machine, / and I'm a man fighting / with myself."

Komunyakaa's approach is very effective. The reader gets a context and then is taken into his inner Vietnam War world. He enriches understanding and then stimulates sensibilities by introducing his experience, in a personal and lyric manner. In this way, the strange horror, the "nightmare geometry" of the Vietnam War is revealed, poem by poem, page by page.

Tim O'Brien uses a similar technique in *The Things They Carried*. In "How to Tell a True War Story", O'Brien uses a "meta-fiction" technique of talking about his approach to writing in the actual story itself. The narrator states:

> A true war story is never moral. It does not instruct, nor encourage virtue, nor suggest models of proper human behavior, nor restrain men from doing the things men have always done. If a story seems moral, do not believe it. If at the end of a war story you feel uplifted, or if you feel that some small bit of rectitude has been salvaged from the larger waste, then you have been made the victim of a very old and terrible lie.
>
> ...
>
> In any war story, especially a true one, it's difficult to separate what happened from what seemed to happen. What seems to happen becomes its own happening and has to be told that way. The angles of vision are skewed.
>
> ...
>
> In many cases, a true war story cannot be believed. If you believe it, be skeptical. It's a question of credibility. Often the crazy stuff is true and the normal stuff isn't, because the normal stuff is necessary to make you believe the truly incredible craziness.

Later in that same story, the "war story" is told by Rat Kiley, who came across a lone baby water buffalo in the mountains and caught it with a rope. Rat tells us:

> He opened up a can of C rations, pork and beans, but the baby buffalo wasn't interested.
>
> Rat shrugged.
>
> He stepped back and shot it through the right front knee. The animal did not make a sound. It went down hard, the got up again, and Rat took careful aim and shot off an ear. He shot it in the hindquarters and in the little hump at its back. He shot it twice in the flanks. It wasn't to kill, it was to hurt. He put the rifle muzzle up against the mouth and shot the mouth away.

O'Brien uses the same changes in psychic distance that Komunyakaa does. He states that war stories if they are real, seem crazy. And then he tells the crazy war story, from the inside, as if it was being recounted to people that were there, who understood even the motivation – not to kill, but to hurt. The shifting of psychic distance in both these books is a key aspect of how they can effectively portray the unusual and strange scene and experience that was the War in Vietnam.

The psychic distance in O'Brien's third person is much closer than Komunyakaa's – so close it seems like a close first person at times. Komunyakaa uses a more lyric and evocative third person that lingers more resolutely but lacks the power of personal testimony. The psychic distance is close, but not too close, leaving unanswered questions that create tension and an emotional hook.

Point of View Layer – "Who Am I? You are Me!"

Point of view is uniquely important for war literature, and especially so for the Vietnam War. In choosing to write with war as a setting, backstory or major theme, the basic questions become critical – "who is telling this story?" and "what did they do versus what did they see?" Authenticity is critical in writing about war and the Vietnam War experience has the added complexity that most American Vietnam War soldiers did things they don't want to admit and saw things they cannot detach from. Classic war writings have had clear, sharp, consistent points of view throughout. This is less prevalent in the writing about the Vietnam War. The shame that many Vietnam War veterans felt and the bizarre reality that was the war itself contributed to the importance of utilizing points of view creatively.

Both *Dien Cai Dau* and *The Things They Carried* are written from multiple points of view. Both start with a collective, second person piece. As noted above, "Camouflaging the Chimera", the opening poem in Komunyakaa's collection, starts in a grounded place, a recounting of the ways that they used foliage on their helmets. It ends in an interior, reflective and slightly surreal place:

> .... ; we held our breath,
>
> > ready to spring the L-shaped
> > ambush, as a world revolved
> > under each man's eyelid.

The transition from reporting in the second person to the more intimate reflection reveals the soldier's experience, a collective experience that gives it weight and authority. They did these things and this is how they experienced them, personally.

The next poem, "Tunnels" is a first-person poem recounting the narrator's thoughts and events about another soldier investigating a village tunnel, imaging what the tunnel rat was experiencing:

> Crawling headfirst down the hole,
> he kicks the air & disappears.
> I feel like I'm down there
> with him, moving ahead, pushed by a river of darkness, …

It is almost a recounting of a personal experience, but not quite. It has the distance afforded by telling someone else's story, but also the closeness that supports lines such as:

> … he knows the pulse
> of mysteries & diversions
> like thoughts trapped in the ground.

The point of view he chooses supports the personal experience and reflection without it being a narrative or reportage. As a poet, Komunyakaa demonstrated considerable skill and attention to point of view in *Dien Cai Dau*. This is part of its unique strength, as poetry is generally assumed to be a first-person form, whether written in the first or third person. Komunyakaa's effective use of multiple points of view delivers a powerful and multi-dimensional view of the American Vietnam War experience. A more limited use of point of view would likely have been less authentic, believable and moving.

Later in the book, the third person is used more extensively. The arms-length point of view pieces address less acceptable, more uniquely "Vietnam experiences" – fragging the Platoon Leader, encounters with prostitutes and the self-immolation of a monk. This change in point of view allows Komunyakaa to convey the bizarre strangeness of the Vietnam War experience in a manner that is understandable but isn't threatening. Toward the end of the volume, Komunyakaa takes on the difficult and recurring trauma of the Vietnam War for American soldiers – coming home. From "Between Days":

> His row of tin soldiers
>
> lines the window sill. The sunset
>
> flashes across them like a blast.
>
> She's buried the Silver Star
>
> & flag under his winter clothes.
>
> ...
>
> Her chair faces the walkway
>
> where she sits before the TV
>
> asleep, as the screen dissolves
>
> into days between the snow.

The point of view allows him to show us what is happening, gives the space for powerful empathy, but does not delve into the strong emotions and conflicts that are being experienced. Komunyakaa was a reporter in the U. S. Army in Vietnam and it is "normal" for him to use a reporting voice. But this is not the same - while the point of view is third person, and somewhat detached, the psychic distance is close. He employs personal objects and details that only could be known by being there, with the narrator.

Tim O'Brien employs multiple points of view in *The Things They Carried*, and in unique ways. While multiple points of view and changes in point of view are more common in fiction, O'Brien uses point of view changes powerfully to manage the stories, individually and as a collection. The entire book is set up as a contract of sorts, between the author and reader. Though the book is called "fiction", the Dedication makes it clear that it is at least partly auto-biographical and there are several chapters where the narrator refers to himself as "Tim", that seem to recount the author's own experiences. O'Brien was a grunt in the Vietnam War, a foot soldier. Most of the book is told in the third person, through the eyes and words of what we are led to believe are O'Brien's patrol buddies. He knows very personal details about them and uses their senses to communicate. From the title story:

> All he could do was dig. He used his entrenching tool like an axe, slashing, feeling both love and hate, and then later, when it was full dark, he sat at the bottom of his foxhole and wept. It went on for a long while. In part, he was grieving for Ted Lavender, but mostly it was for Martha, and for himself, because she belonged to another world, which was not quite real, and because she was a junior at Mount Sebastian College in New Jersey, a poet and a virgin and uninvolved, and because he realized she did not love him and never would.

In this section, the narrator seems to know everything that is going on for the person he is discussing (Lieutenant Jimmy Cross) – feelings, thoughts and passions. The reader has no reason to believe that the narrator does not know everything there is to know about Jimmy Cross, at that moment, in that space. This is a very close third person narration with an intimate psychic distance. It is hard to imagine that anything is lost by it not being written in the first person.

Elsewhere in *The Things They Carried*, the point of view changes, more so in the later part of the book. O'Brien uses an approach different from Komunyakaa's third person, reporting point of view – first person plural, usually the collective "we" and "us" except when dialogue is employed. From the story "Style":

> There was no music. Most of the hamlet had burned down, including her house, which was now smoke, and the girl danced with her eyes half closed, her feet bare. She was maybe fourteen. She had black hair and brown skin. "Why's she dancing?" Azar said. We searched through the wreckage, but there wasn't much to find.
>
> ...
>
> When we dragged them out, the girl kept dancing. She put the palms of her hands against her ears, which must have meant something, and she danced sideways for a short while...

The effect is to make the personal experiences in the stories, shared experiences - we did this, we anticipated that. There is a sharing of shame and guilt coupled with the underscored validation that it was seen others, not just the narrator. As if to say, "These were horrific events and it wasn't just me that experienced them, we did."

Komunyakaa utilizes a similar first person plural device occasionally, as in "Communique" which recounts a Bob Hope show:

> Bob Hope's on stage, but we want the Gold Diggers,
>   want a flash of legs
> through the hemorrhage of vermillion, giving us
>   something to kill for.
> We want our hearts wrung out like rags & ground down
>   to Georgia dust

The parts in *The Things They Carried* that are clearly first-person singular are personal reflections. The story "Love", recounts a reunion with Jimmy Cross, one of his patrol:

> At one point, I remember we paused over a snapshot of Ted Lavender, and after a while, Jimmy rubbed his eyes and said he'd never forgiven himself for Lavender's death. It was something that would never go away, he said quietly, and I nodded and told him I felt the same about certain things.

O'Brien's choice of point of view controls the story's perspective. He employs several different points of view that shape the portrayal of the strangeness and complexities. While less reflective and grounded in describing some of the War's horrors than Komunyakaa, O'Brien is also less personally engaged in the first person throughout. There are several places where it is unclear whether O'Brien is describing himself, what he saw, what he imagined or what someone told him. This is purposeful, but at times confusing.

Both writers utilize several points of view for much of their writing in these two books. While generally uncharacteristic, especially for writing about war, this allows them to reveal the surreal and complex experiences of the Vietnam War and to create focus and provide space for understanding and clarity. In both works, the multiple views not only provide a richer context, they also create a literary tension and energy that supports their authenticity. And, possibly, provided both Vietnam War veterans with the freedom and space they needed to write.

"So What?"

The challenge in writing about the Vietnam War experience is significant. Lorrie Smith, in *Fourteen Landing Zones: Approaches to Vietnam War Literature* summarized it:

> In many ways, veterans of the Vietnam War share a similar position with women and ethnic minorities: mute, invisible, objectified by the dominant culture, blamed for circumstances which in fact have victimized them. Writers in this position necessarily find an authentic voice by resisting the cultural codes that define them as other, and they necessarily challenge prevailing norms.

It was a horrific experience, a shock to the system for most soldiers and a trauma that lingers still, beyond America and in those that were there. Writing about the Vietnam War in an impactful and lasting way, that speaks to those who did not serve and authentically for those who did, is a challenge, even for gifted writers who were there. *Dien Cai Dau* and *The Things They Carried* utilize point of view, in concert with psychic distance and language, to create just such an authentic and realistic experience. Komunyakaa and O'Brien's use colloquial, genuine language, changes in psychic distance and multiple points of view to recreate the experience in a way that manages this tension between authenticity and accessibility. Both made the experience of combat Vietnam War soldiers real and understandable. In doing so, they served a broader community and more important need than what we did while serving in country.

Works Cited

Andrews, Michael, and David Widup. *In Country.* Bombshelter Press, 1994.

Barth, R. L. *A Soldier's Time: Vietnam War Poems.* J. Daniel, 1988.

Ehrhart, W. D. "Soldier-Poets of the Vietnam War." *Virginia Quarterly Review*, vol. 63, no. 2, 1987, pp. 246–265.

Ehrhart, W. D. *To Those Who Have Gone Home Tired: New & Selected Poems.* Thunder's Mouth Press, 1984.

Gilman, Owen W., and Smith Lorrie, editors. *America Rediscovered: Critical Essays on Literature and Film of the Vietnam War.* Garland, 1990.

Jason, Philip K. *Fourteen Landing Zones: Approaches to Vietnam War Literature.* University of Iowa Press, 1991.

Komunyakaa, Yusef. *Dien Cai Dau.* Wesleyan University Press, 1988.

Mahony, Phillip, editor. *From Both Sides Now: The Poetry of the Vietnam War and Its Aftermath.* Scribner Poetry, 1998.

Marshall, Kathryn. *In the Combat Zone: An Oral History of American Women in Vietnam.* Little, Brown and Company, 1987.

O'Brien, Tim. *The Things They Carried.* Mariner Books, 2009.

Rottmann, Larry, et al., editors. *Winning Hearts and Minds: War Poems by Vietnam Veterans.* 1st Casualty Press, 1972.

Weigl, Bruce. *Song of Napalm.* Grove Atlantic, 2001.

PART III
BIBLIOGRAPHY

MFA in Writing List

1. Abani, Christopher. *Sanctificum*. Copper Canyon Press, 2010.
2. Addonizio, Kim, and Dorianne Laux. *The Poet's Companion: A Guide to the Pleasures of Writing Poetry*. W.W. Norton, 1997.
3. Alcosser, Sandra. *Except by Nature*. Graywolf Press, 1998.
4. Anderson, Doug. *The Moon Reflected Fire: Poems*. Alice James Books, 1994.
5. Ashbery, John. *Where Shall I Wander: New Poems*. Ecco, 2006.
6. Bass, Ellen. *Like a Beggar*. Copper Canyon Press, 2014.
7. Bell, Marvin. *The Book of the Dead Man*. Copper Canyon Press, 1994.
8. ----- Nightworks: Poems 1962-2000 (Second Edition). Copper Canyon Press, 2002.
9. Berryman, John. *77 Dream Songs*. Farrar, Straus & Giroux, 1978.
10. Bishop, Elizabeth. *Poems*. Chatto & Windus, 2011.
11. Bukowski, Charles. Love Is a Dog from Hell: Poems 1974-1977. Ecco, 2003.
12. Chiasson, Dan. *Bicentennial: Poems*. Knopf, 2014.
13. Clifton, Lucille. *Blessing the Boats: New and Selected Poems, 1988-2000*. BOA Editions, 2008.
14. Collins, Billy. *Rain in Portugal*. Picador, 2017.
15. Corral, Eduardo C. *Slow Lightning: Poems*. Yale University Press, 2012.
16. Corso, Gregory. *The Happy Birthday of Death*. New Directions Publishing Corporation, 1960.
17. D., H., and Aliki Barnstone. *Trilogy*. New Directions, 1998.
18. Dawes, Kwame Senu Neville. *Duppy Conqueror: New and Selected Poems*. Edited by Matthew Shenoda, Copper Canyon Press, 2013.
19. Ehrhart, W. *To Those Who Have Gone Home Tired: New & Selected Poems*. Thunder's Mouth Press, 1984.
20. Erdrich, Louise. *Baptism of Desire: Poems*. Harper, 2001.
21. Fairchild, B. H. *The Art of the Lathe*. Alice James Books, 1998.
22. Flynn, Nick. *Some Ether*. Graywolf Press, 2000.
23. Forché, Carolyn. *The Angel of History*. HarperPerennial, 1994.

24. Francis, Vievee. *Forest Primeval: Poems*. Northwestern Univ. Press, 2016.

25. Gaspar, Frank. *Night of a Thousand Blossoms*. Alice James Books, 2004.

26. Glück, L. *The Wild Iris*. W.W. Norton & Company Ltd, 1996.

27. Graham, Jorie. *Overlord: Poems*. HarperCollins, 2005.

28. Hamill, Sam. *Nootka Rose: Poems*. Breitenbush Books, 1987.

29. Harrison, Jim. *Dead Man's Float*. Copper Canyon Press, 2016.

30. Hirshfield, Jane. *The Beauty: Poems*. Alfred A. Knopf, 2017.

31. Hirshfield, Jane. *Nine Gates: Entering the Mind of Poetry: Essays*. HarperPerennial, 1998.

32. Jarrell, Randall. "War Poems." *The Complete Poems*, Farrar, Straus and Giroux, 1969, pp. 143–197.

33. Jones, Richard. *At Last We Enter Paradise*. Copper Canyon Press, 1991.

34. Justice, Donald. *Collected Poems*. Alfred A. Knopf, 2016.

35. Kaminsky, Ilya. *Dancing in Odessa*. Arc, 2014.

36. Karr, Mary. *Tropic of Squalor Poems*. HarperCollins, 2018.

37. Kay, Sarah. *No Matter the Wreckage: Poems*. Write Bloody Publishing, America's Independent Press, 2014.

38. Kinnell, Galway. *Mortal Acts, Mortal Words*. Houghton Mifflin, 1980.

39. Knight, Etheridge. *The Essential Etheridge Knight*. University of Pittsburgh Press, 2012.

40. Knott, Bill. *I Am Flying into Myself: Selected Poems*, 1960-2014. Farrar, Straus and Giroux, 2017.

41. Komunyakaa, Yusef. *Dien Cai Dau*. Wesleyan University Press, 1988.

42. ----- *Neon Vernacular: New and Selected Poems*. Wesleyan University Press, 1993.

43. Kunitz, Stanley. *Passing through: The Later Poems*, New and Selected. W.W. Norton, 1997.

44. Lai, Thanhha. *Inside Out & Back Again*. HarperCollins, 2013.

45. Laux, Dorianne. *The Book of Men: Poems*. W.W. Norton, 2012.

46. ----- *Facts about the Moon: Poems*. W.W. Norton, 2007.

47. Lee, David. *Driving and Drinking: A Poem.* Copper Canyon Press, 2004.

48. ----- Last Call. Wings Press, 2014.

49. Lee, Li-Young. *The City in Which I Love You: Poems.* BOA Ed., 2010.

50. ----- Rose. BOA Editions, Ltd., 1986.

51. Levertov, Denise. *To Stay Alive.* New Directions Publ. Corp., 1971.

52. Levine, Philip. *They Feed They Lion; &, the Names of the Lost.* Knopf, 1999.

53. Lifshin, Lyn. *A Girl Goes into the Woods: Selected Poems.* NYQ Books, 2013.

54. Logan, John. *Spring of the Thief; Poems,* 1960-1962. Knopf, 1963.

55. Mahony, Phillip, editor. *From Both Sides Now: The Poetry of the Vietnam War and Its Aftermath.* Scribner Poetry, 1998.

56. Merwin, W. S. *The Moon before Morning.* Copper Canyon Press, 2015.

57. Millar, Joseph. *Kingdom.* Carnegie Mellon University Press, 2017.

58. Neruda, Pablo, and Alastair Reid. *Extravagaria:* Translated by Alastair Reid. Farrar, Straus and Giroux, 1974.

59. O'Brien, Tim. *The Things They Carried.* Mariner Books, 2009.

60. Olds, Sharon. *Odes.* Alfred A. Knopf, 2016.

61. ----- *Stag's Leap.* Alfred A. Knopf, 2015.

62. Oliver, Mary. House of Light: Beacon Press, 1990.

63. ----- *Upstream: Selected Essays.* Penguin Press, 2016.

64. Orr, David. B*eautiful & Pointless: A Guide to Modern Poetry.* Harper Perennial, 2012.

65. Pessoa, Fernando. *Fernando Pessoa & Co.: Selected Poems.* Translated by Richard Zenith, Grove Press, 1998.

66. Rottmann, Larry, et al. *Winning Hearts and Minds: War Poems by Vietnam Veterans.* 1st Casualty Press, 1972.

67. Sexton, Anne. *Complete Poems.* Houghton Mifflin Company, 1981.

68. Shange, Ntozake. *For Colored Girls Who Have Considered Suicide/When the Rainbow Is Enuf: a Choreopoem.* Scribner, 1975.

69. Simic, Charles, and Mark Strand. *Another Republic: 17 European and South American Writers.* Ecco Press, 2008.

70. Snyder, Gary. *No Nature: New and Selected Poems.* Pantheon Books, 1993.

71. Soto, Gary. *Who Will Know Us?: New Poems.* Chronicle Books, 1990.

72. Stafford, William. *Writing the Australian Crawl: Views on the Writer's Vocation.* Univ. of Michigan Pr., 1989.

73. Tate, James. *Dome of the Hidden Pavilion: New Poems.* Ecco, an Imprint of HarperCollinsPublishers, 2016.

74. Tranströmer, Tomas, and Robert Bly. *The Half-Finished Heaven: The Best Poems of Tomas Tranströmer.* Graywolf Press, 2001.

75. Turner, Brian. Here, Bullet. Alice James Books, 2005.

76. Wallace, George. *Smashing Rock and Straight as Razors.* Blue Light Press, 2017.

77. Webb, Charles Harper. *Brain Camp.* University of Pittsburgh Press, 2015.

78. Weigl, Bruce. *Song of Napalm.* Grove Atlantic, 2001.

79. Whitman, Walt. *Walt Whitman's Civil War.* Edited by Walter Lowenfels, Da Capo Press, 1989.

80. Williams, C. K. *Flesh and Blood.* Farrar, Straus and Giroux, 1987.

David Widup lives in Ashland, Oregon. He is a poet, coach and editor who has authored two books of poetry, several chapbooks. David's poetry has also appeared in various literary journals including *ACM*, *Rattle*, *ONTHEBUS* and *ZZYVA*. He holds an MFA in Creative Writing program from Pacific University.